PIECES OF ME ALL OVER THE PLACE

PIECES OF ME ALL OVER THE PLACE

ASHANTI "TAY LASHEA" FLEMISTER

J. Merrill
PUBLISHING

J Merrill Publishing, Inc., Columbus 43207
www.JMerrill.pub

Library of Congress Control Number: 2020923848
ISBN-13: 978-1-950719-68-6 (Paperback)
ISBN-13: 978-1-950719-67-9 (eBook)

Title: Pieces of Me All Over the Place
Author: Ashanti Flemister
Photographs: Kei Imagery

I dedicate this book to my Lord and Savior, Jesus Christ, who has always been the glue that holds my brokenness together.

I know that just being me disappoints you at times, but I thank you for loving me and always putting me back together even when my own freewill tends to shatter me into pieces.

You are the only one who truly makes me whole, and I am grateful for all the visible cracks of my life as they are living testimonies of victory.

I also dedicate this book to my family and friends who believed in me even when I didn't believe in myself. You know who you are, and I just want to say thank you. I love you, dearly!

CONTENTS

Introduction

Pieces Of Me All Over The Place is self-exclamatory. It is a poetic journey of many pieces of my life covering the highs, lows, love, heartache, spiritual and life lessons. I have used poetry, music, and God as sources of healing and a positive way to escape from anxiety and depression.

It took a long time to complete this book because I had lost my passion for writing it. I had writer's block and had been overwhelmed with pursuing my Master's Degree in Social Work and surviving the pandemic of Covid-19! What an emotional roller coaster! I hope this book will be an inspiration to some of you to keep pressing and pursue your dreams no matter what!

Am I Good Enough

BY ASHANTI FLEMISTER

Am I good enough for you
Or am I something less
I promise that when I'm with you
I will give you the best

You wouldn't understand what
I'm all about
If you don't have the dignity
To turn me inside out

I want to get to know you
But I'm kind of scared
The anxiety of getting rejected is
Fluttering through the air

I know that I may not be as pretty
As Halle Berry
But I know that it takes more than looks
To get to know me

If you take the time to see what's inside
You will be in for a big surprise
So, use your heart and not your eyes

B.H.B.

BY ASHANTI FLEMISTER

Chocolate with Locs of Glory
Oh his dark brown skin tells a story
About Hip Hop
The way he pop, locks, drops,
And tick tocks
Will mesmerize your mind each
Time that he move
Now let's not forget the way he grooves
Behind the wheels of steel and
Keeps the party jumpin'
With each scratch and scribble
He commands the rhythm
That beat as if it is
So simple to make
The crowd get lit
Have you seen his crew?
B-boy styling under his
Directions since they
Were about two

His heart is big and he's
Always looking out for others
They call him B.H.B.
Brother's Helping Brothers

Blame It on Me

BY ASHANTI FLEMISTER

Blame me for loving you
Blame me for still having grown
Woman feelings and playing the fool
Blame me for not hating you

The way that you treated me could have
Made me despise you
And deny you like you have done to me
I asked the Lord multiple times to

Take these feeling away because I don't
Belong to you
Yet my heart is confused
After three long years
My mind, body, and spirit won't
Let you go

Blame me for wanting to do right by you
Blame me for wanting to
Hold you down forever

For wanting to wipe your tears from
Your eyes when some else has hurt you

Blame me for wanting to rub your back
For wanting to hold you and kiss you
As if you were truly mine
Seems like we always fuss, cuss, and dismiss each other
Then we're back to that same ol' grind

Blame me for telling the truth about the way I feel.
Blame me for loving you for real
Now blame me for finally lifting my head up high
And finally walking away

Blame me for letting go and saying goodbye
To another gloomy day
Because you don't love me
There is no reciprocity
So, blame me for claiming back my dignity
And declaring that these feelings for you
Are now history

Blame me

Broken Vessel

BY ASHANTI FLEMISTER

Growing up, I never realized the value that was within me
Broken and disgusted trying to be set free

From the terror that awaited me when I opened up
My big brown eyes
A mirror image of me as the enemy stared
At me with a shallow sigh

No one could see my tears or feel my pain
Since my loved ones had problems of their own
They couldn't tell the sunshine from the rain

Years ago, I thought I found love
Someone who I thought loved me
Three years I kissed good-bye
Because he didn't see me or feel me

As if I wasn't there
I couldn't blame him, though, because he was so unaware
That I was broken inside

So he could only love the surface
This thing called love seemed to be worthless

On my own again
Accumulated male friends
My vessel became theirs
I traded it for what I needed within

So broken, used, and abused
Played like a fool
But at last, the Sovereign Almighty God
Led me to the truth

Jesus' light had overtaken my darkness
Although I've fallen many times
I fight myself daily to stay focused
And ignore the enemy's lies

Sometimes my past tries to hunt me and stop me
But mercy says no
My very life is depended on thee
So, I won't let go

I thank Jesus for loving me in spite of my ways
And for choosing this broken vessel to follow Him
For the rest of my days.

Closer to You

BY ASHANTI FLEMISTER

I remember when I was so lost in sin
But you saved my soul, and You took me in
No other friend can do me like You do
I could've given up a long time ago
But You showed me that all things were possible
If I seek You and only You
Then I should make it through
But sometimes, my burdens get me down
And You seem so far away
So, can You show me how
And tell me how
I could get closer to You today
Show me how
Tell me how
I need to know
how I could get
Closer to you
Closer to You,
Closer to You Jesus
When I decided to accept you in my heart

I was destined for a brand-new start
I longed to be a reflection of You
Nobody said that the road would be easy
And when the enemy is trying to defeat me
You said if I live Your Word
And Do Your Word
And I should be closer
To You today

Confessions from an Independent Black Woman

BY ASHANTI FLEMISTER

Black King
I need you
Now don't get it twisted because my father
Had raised me to be independent, but I can't front
Although it may look like I have it going on
On my own
It gets hard trying to carry the weight of
This world solo
And I can't help to be lost in a daze
Daydreaming about how it would be
To be your Queen, to be
Your wifey, the mother of your children
Your personal chef, your rib,
Yep, your very own help meet

Black King
I desire you
Although some of the images that you portray
Makes me cringe in my skin
Such as pants saggin' like lil'

Boys in the hood
On the street corner up to no good
I can't help but to have a sweet tooth
For an assortment of chocolate
A craving for a manly black man
Can I talk about it?
I'm talking tall, stalky,
Nicely trimmed beard, sideburns aligned
Neat locs, tight fade, a banging smile
And pretty brown eyes
You make a sista wanna say
THANK YA!
For the view
I love me some Black Men
Sistas, I don't know about you

Black King
I'm waiting for you to get in position
To take the lead and show me that there is no completion
Yet some of you will give your body and soul away
To anything that has legs and a vagina
Your homeboys claim that you are a playa
But some of you are simply fine China
Trying to fill a void
And you think what better way
To mend your broken heart but to have
Multiple play toys
In your iPhone or Androids

Black King
You need to understand that I'm worth it
Your love, that's right
I'm worth it
I'm not a dime piece because I'm priceless
I can't be laid away or thrifted
My value is worth too much

To settle to just be your Friends with Benefits

Black King
Contrary to what you may believe
I've been ready to submit
But I need to know without a shadow of a doubt
That your love is legit
And that against all odds
You would protect me
I handle my own grown woman business
So, you don't have to worry
What's mine can ultimately be yours
I'm a Black Queen but wait, there's more

Black King
I want to love you unconditionally
Until death do us part
But I need you to know without a shadow of a doubt
That you are ready to make me number 1
In your heart

Created to Worship You

BY ASHANTI FLEMISTER

Chorus
I worship, I worship, I worship you.... Jesus 2x

Verse 1
I was created to worship You
Worship You
In spirit and in truth
I was created to worship You
Worship You
In Spirit and in truth
Worship you

Chorus
I worship, I worship, I worship you.... Jesus 2x

Breakdown
And I was created to worship you

Instrumental

Verse 2
If anybody wants to know why I do...what I do
I do it to worship you
If anybody wants to know why I do...what I do
I do it to worship you

Bridge
Worship is more than a simple hand raise
A lifestyle of living lifting up Jesus' name
Mind is renewed as well as your soul
Giving up your life and allowing God to take control

Crush

BY ASHANTI FLEMISTER

He has an intellectual state of mind
He dresses so nice
Yes, he's so damn fine

His voice sounds smooth and slightly
deep when he speaks
He snores loudly when he is in a deep sleep

His hair is dark brown, curly, afro style
Every time I see him, he drives me wild
His skin is sexy chocolate, smooth when touched
I guess that's why I think about him so much

Emotional Rollercoaster

BY ASHANTI FLEMISTER

It's funny how women get shunned for feeling this way, but I thank God that I have male friends who aren't ashamed to say that they have felt this way before. You might not hear this at the Barbershop, though...

I wrote a poem about it... wanna hear it... here it goes... LOL!

Enjoy....

Emotional Rollercoaster

Is it alright to feel
Is it alright to cry
Is it alright to feel pain
When your heart has been denied

Is it alright to feel empty
When they don't feel the same way
Is it alright to be happy one minute
And feel sad at the end of the day

Just another emotional roller coaster
That you tried to avoid
One moment you feel like you gave them love
The next moment you feel like their toy

You try to process your feelings
But they just don't make any sense
Just another emotional coaster
Because true love didn't ever exist

Forever More

BY ASHANTI FLEMISTER

Verse 1
I've spent like most of my days
Most of my nights
Waiting to hear from you
I've been through plenty of disappointments
But it's been worth since I have you
It takes a minute to get it right
And I thank You, Lord, for making a change in my life
Washed me clean of my iniquities
Renewed my mine so I could love You right
And all I want to do is love you

Chorus
All I want to do is love you
And give you a lifetime of happiness
All I want to do is please you
And give you joy and so much more
Forevermore...do do do do do do do do do
Forevermore...do do do do do do do do do

Verse 2
Don't need anybody else's attention
Just want to spend my life loving you
Give you the best years of my life
You're the that I gave my heart to

Repeat Chorus

Forgiven

BY ASHANTI FLEMISTER

Seems like I've been orbiting in "outer space"
In desperate need of the Lord
To put me back into His Place
Of refuge...rescue me, Lord.

Seems like I've gone way too far
Mind is cloudy
Spirit is willing
Body is discombobulated...I mean really...

This again I see
So what lesson is behind all this mess?
Yes, it's me; oh Lord again
Standing in the need of prayer

So, what the deal
Trying to make sense of how I feel
In distress
Failed yet another test

Who would truly understand
Life is like a rubber band
Trials may stretch it
But God's grace is sufficient

And will make your life
Bounce back to its original position
Shame is my middle name
I'm not fit to play this game

Is this part of my mission
Although I don't deserve it
You said, "Forgiven."

Fortress

BY ASHANTI FLEMISTER

Wrap me in your arms, Jesus
Shield me from the aftermath of my own emotions
As my heart desires unconditional love
That should've been established since birth

That love from a mother's womb
From childhood to adulthood
Had somehow gotten lost
And caused confusion in my identity and made me question my worth

Hide me from my desire to seek it from men
Keep me from giving myself away
To settle for the pleasure of the innermost passion of a secret sin

Remind me that there is no greater love than your own
My life bears the fruit of your love song

Because I'm still here.
In spite of my wicked ways and deceitful desires
You are the wind beneath my wings

My eternal flame of a bomb fire

Hold me, lord
Keep me from meeting and greeting tragedy
Because of my refusal to patiently wait
Protect me from the demons of my past
Who remind me of self-hate

Cover me from the monsoon of longing to be wanted
That overtakes my heart
Help me to be patient and to not be weary
So that I won't fall apart

Mold me to be that virtuous wife
So that I can be ready when you see it fit
For my true love to arrive
And to open his eyes to help him notice me
So that he won't pass me by

Friend

BY ASHANTI FLEMISTER

You've been there through tragedies that I thought I couldn't get
through
You always see the positive in all the struggles that I battled
You've always lent a hand just from giving me your ear
You've been my life coach for so many years

You've been a constant friend, although I've gotten on your last nerves
You've dealt with my mood swings and all my drama like a soap opera
You've made me laugh when my world was drowning in tears

I probably told you before, but from of my heart I just want to say
thank you
For being my friend all these years

Get it together, Love God

BY ASHANTI FLEMISTER

You know my name, and I heard you call me a thousand times
When you suffer from pain and anguish
Desperately pleading for a reason why
You feel like I don't love you because of the things that I had put you
through
My advice to you is simply stop complaining
Because in the midst of the storm, I was there for you, maintaining

But you put your trust in man
When things get rough
I'm your healer, your provider, your more than enough
But when things don't go your way, it's my name that you curse
Then you have the nerve to put down my children
You know those folks in the church

You don't understand my ways because you fail to study my word
There are some things that you know about me
But you still act like you haven't heard
Please understand that I love you and I am concerned
Take heed, change your attitude, and acknowledge my statutes

Believe in me and my son Jesus
Who will be your guide to the truth

Have you been looking at the world lately
It's not getting any better
My Son is coming back
So please get it together

Have Faith

BY ASHANTI FLEMISTER

He could do exceedingly above anything that you could ever imagine
Just have faith believe, and He'll come through
Be still and watch Him make it happen
Have Faith
Have Faith
Have Faith
Just Have Faith

There are times that you may be feeling down
And you feel like you cannot go on
Lift your head up high to the sky
And watch Jesus make a change in your life

Have Faith
Have Faith
Have Faith
Just Have Faith

Heal the Part that Hurts

BY ASHANTI FLEMISTER

Heal the part that hurts (Oh Lord. Oh, Oh)
Release me the chains that are binding me (Oh, Oh)
Heal the part that hurts (Oh Lord. Oh, Oh)
Release me from my past and set me free
I just want to be free
I just want to be free

Free to love again
Free to trust again
Free to let go
Free to let God take control

I want to be free
I just want to be free

Free to make my own mistakes
Free to learn from them
Free to release
Free to give all my problems to Him
I want to be free

I just want to be free

Heal the part that hurts (Oh Lord. Oh Oh)
Release me from the chains that are binding me (Oh Oh)
Heal the part that hurts (Oh Lord. Oh Oh)
Release me from the past and set me free
I just want to be free
I just want to be free

I'm Just Me

BY ASHANTI FLEMISTER

I've been misunderstood for years
Almost like forever
I lived under the shadow of
What people perceive me to be
I mean whatever
I'm just me
A loner trying to make
It in this world
With a purpose
Use my creativity
As an outlet
Trying my best to stay focus
But I continue to be distracted
By my own insecurities
Lusting after the things
That are toxic for me
Been trying to find love
But love hasn't been
That fond to me
Emotional roller coaster

Coasting out of control
Where it stops
The hell if I know
I'm just me
Crossed so many people
For speaking my mind
A little too freely
However, I have given
Myself away constantly
To my blood
To my friends
To undeserved men
Like when is somebody
Going to see
That I need to be rescued
That I need to be loved unconditionally
I'm tired of apologizing for knowing who I am
I'm a grown-ass woman
Who made plenty of mistakes
And some mistakes
I continue to make
Until I say that I'm done...done
Sometimes being me ain't no fun
But I have to get up every morning
To look at myself in the mirror
Giving other people's opinions
About me, a welcoming middle finger
Because this is who you came to see
And I am that I am
And I shall
Always be just me.

I am free

BY ASHANTI FLEMISTER

Who the Son sets free is surely free indeed
There is victory in Him
Therefore, there is victory inside of me.
I'm no longer a slave to my sins
Christ's blood has washed me squeaky clean
My past doesn't define me, although haters try to remind me but
From my own self-conscience thoughts
Confidence manifested as I stride
Giving my problems to Jesus Christ
I swallow my pride because
I am free

My enemies can't no longer hide me
Break me down or bind me
Handcuff me or tie me
Haters don't even try me because
I am free

To forgive and let go

Allowing God to take control
Who the Son set's free is free indeed
There is victory in Him
Therefore, there is victory inside of me because
I AM FREE

I Learned

BY ASHANTI FLEMISTER

I have finally gotten to a place where
I learned to love you unselfishly
There have been nights
that I wept for you
Wishing that I could be there for you
but the only thing that
I could do was pray
Dear Heavenly Father, bless him
Continue to shape and mold him
To the man that you
have predestined him to be
Heal him
Love on him
So that he could be all that
You have called him to be
Help him to know his purpose
and walk out his true destiny
I finally learned how
to love you unselfishly

By letting go
And desiring your happiness
Even when you're not with me

I'm Not Worthy

BY ASHANTI FLEMISTER

I don't deserve your grace, but somehow you continue to love me
anyway.
I don't deserve another breath or to see the light of another day
With opened arms, you welcome me back again and again and again
I don't deserve your grace, but you're a constant friend.
No matter how far I go, your spirit is with me.
Nothing can separate me from the love of you.
Even when I'm lost, you always see me through.
Oh, Jesus, why you love me so.
You said you will never leave me or forsake me
Even when I want to leave
I'm nothing without you because you are the air that I breathe.
If I was you, I would've been let myself go.
I'm not worthy, but for some reason, you think so...

Incredible Jesus

BY ASHANTI FLEMISTER

Lord, You are Incredible
You healed the sick and raised the dead
So many miracles You've performed
You are the Son of Man

Lord, You are wonderful
You died on the cross, and You shed Your blood
To save the souls of mankind
There is no greater love

Lord, You are excellent
A perfect sacrifice to save souls
For all mankind
You gave up Your Holy Spirit
To lead us in the truth and the light

My Jesus, You are magnificent
For every knee shall bow
And every tongue will confess Your name

You are the true and living God
There is no other name that we could claim

It takes Time

BY ASHANTI FLEMISTER

It takes time to trust again after being betrayed once
It takes time to love again
after loving someone too much
It takes time to learn the lessons from
all of the hurt and sorrow
It takes time to understand when it rains and pours
the sun is destined to come out tomorrow
It takes time to accept someone else's imperfections
When you can't accept your own
It takes time to appreciate someone's time
When you have never spent time alone
So, don't lose heart and don't rush
Patience has never been a crime
Just realize that all things in life
Including love takes time

Let the Lord Take Control

BY ASHANTI FLEMISTER

Lord knows I've been struggling
Feels like I'm going to lose my mind
Doesn't seem like nobody in this world
Could help me out this time
I'm sitting here waiting
For someone to get me out of this hole
Until I decided to let the Lord take control
Throw up my hand and let it all go
Let God be the author of my life
And let His will flow

Said I've been sick
And I couldn't get well
The doctor said there was no cure
My Jesus is a healer, and that's for sure
I took it to the Lord in prayer
And I just want to let you know
My body has been healed
Because I had let the Lord take control

Love Doesn't Make Any Sense

BY ASHANTI FLEMISTER

I can't explain how I feel
My heart yearns for you
But the logic in my mind
Keeps telling me that
This isn't real

My heart reaches out with open arms
But my lips have uttered words
Of negativity and harm
Because you remind me of my previous pain
Crying monsoon of showers that
Only my tear ducts can explain

I feel you in my spirit
Clanging cymbals, kick drum thumps
But reality just doesn't want to hear it
If it was real love, then wouldn't it

Be worth the fight
My mind wants to let you go

But my heart wants to hold on tight
What have you done to me

Seems like our drama
Has become a suspense
I guess this is why people say
That love doesn't make any sense

Move Forward

BY ASHANTI FLEMISTER

There was a time in your life that you felt you couldn't go on
So tired of the continuous struggle.
But with faith and determination
You were able to see the light at the end of the tunnel

You persevered through it all
And you didn't give up on this test
You had to lay your pride to the side
And realized that strength in numbers worked best

Yes, you have made some mistakes
But you are not the only one
They may talk about your past but
Who cares

A new chapter in life has just begun
You made a decision
You lived, and you learned
You're influential now

You've paved the way
For someone else to say
Because of him/her
I can do it

It's my time
It's my turn
So, don't let your yesterday
Dictate your tomorrow

Remember to stay empowered
Keep pressing on and move forward

No More

BY ASHANTI FLEMISTER

I didn't want to fight anymore
So instead of participating in
yet another physical altercation
I fell to the floor
No more

To my surprise, I had seen
The designs of socks wrapped
Around my ankles
As he proudly drug me

Out of the door
With no shoes on my feet
I frantically knocked on
My neighbor's door

She answered and the
Fright in my eyes had
Seemed to remind me of
Something that was familiar

Yes, I do remember the thumps and the
Screams that came through the walls
Of my neighbors' door
She said, "I know"

And she immediately
Gave me the phone
I called the cops on the man
Who I had once called
The love of my life
Because I couldn't take it anymore
No more

I had enough
I just wanted my stuff
Po Po had asked me if I wanted to
Press charges, but although
My next set of emotions was hate
I couldn't imagine him being taken
Away in handcuffs
I just wanted my stuff

This almost was fight number four
I grabbed my things and walked out the door
I thank God that I had the strength and
The courage to say for the last time
No more

Not the One

BY ASHANTI FLEMISTER

It seems like you could see right through me
You know what I need, and I wish that you could give it to me
But in your mind, you think I'm not the one for you
And when you think about us, you seem so confused
All I know is how you make me feel when we're together
And when you hold me in your arms, you make me feel better
I knew that it was best for us to just take our time
But things went pretty fast after one night
And I'm saying to myself that I never should've kissed you
And I never should've spent the night with you
Because I feel like I love you and I
Don't know what to do
Now you're saying to yourself that you never
Should've kissed me
And you never should've made love to me
Because you're feeling so confused
And you don't know what to do
Now my heart wants to give you love
And every night, you're the one that I'm thinking of
But you're not ready for a brand-new love affair

It's going to take some time to even go there again
Now you told me to accept this thing for what it was
Two friends with benefits of making love
And I never was the type to put up a front
But it hurts deep inside that I'm not what you want

One Sided

BY ASHANTI FLEMISTER

You played a melody in my heart
You sang a dream to my mind
Your smile had given me life
Right from the very start
I don't know your purpose
Or the lesson behind this
But I loved you unconditionally
You were so beautiful to me but
You had failed to see me
Things between us were about to come to an end
I had allowed you to use me
And disrespect me
You had the nerve to call me your friend
Now you know that I don't play
When it comes to being disrespected
We would rise, and then we would fall
Because your mouth, you never checked it
It burns my heart whenever I'm in your presence
Because you would just walk on by
Like you didn't know me

I guess we are on that petty
I've moved on, but for some crazy reason
You are still dear to my heart
We did have a connection, but you have
Somehow forgotten that part
But at least now I know the truth
I was only your friend
When it was convenient for you
At your disposal
Anything that I could do
To make your feel good
There I was, your Superwoman
At your rescue
But now I know better
I'm at peace with the fact that we couldn't
Possibly be together
Especially when my needs were being neglected
I deserve better than being rejected

Our Own Demise

BY ASHANTI FLEMISTER

Drug deals, blood spills
to obtain money,
Power and respect
Another black life lost
Another black finger on the trigger
To show whose boss

Black Lives do matter
But they can't tell
Another dead black man walking
And the other one in jail

We're quick to belittle our own race
When another black face just simply walks by
Ready to raise a fist at any defense
Or kill at will, and we wonder why

They think that our Black lives don't have any value
Jealousy, Envy, Failure to squash beef quickly
Take a look in the mirror

We are our own worst enemies

We don't support one another
Instead, we smack our teeth
And think of another competition
I'm not supporting them unless
I'm getting a percentage

Reality TV has made a mockery of our Black Lives
Seems like Love and Hip Hop has become the
New family ties
I mean, what better way to raise a family
But to have eight kids from 4 baby mamas
2 girlfriends and a wife

Popular for the drama
To get that top dollar
Black people, can't you see it starts with us
We need to get better at loving ourselves
And each other, in God we Trust

Each one, reach one,
Let's help each other break generational curses
Cease the Black on Black Crime
And stop putting each other in hearses

Let's stop talking about it
And be about while there is still time
So that we could discontinue being the number one reason
For our own demise

Perfect Peace

BY ASHANTI FLEMISTER

He will keep you in perfect peace if you keep your mind stayed on Him
You don't have to worry about tomorrow
Just let Him do His will

You got laid off from the job
Bills are overdue
No food on the table
You don't know what to do
Just get on your knees and pray
Jesus will make a way
Keep your mind on Him
And make way for brighter days

He will keep you in perfect peace if you keep your mind stayed on Him
You don't have to worry about tomorrow
Just let Him do His will

You've been feeling all alone
Depressed and can't go on
People keep letting you down

Let me tell you about a friend I found
His name is Jesus Christ
And He will make a way
Keep your mind on Him
And make way for brighter days

Play for me

BY ASHANTI FLEMISTER

Can you play for me?
Play a simple melody like you used to make me fall asleep
Practice for 8 hours straight
Until your fingers ached
Can you play for me
Play a simple melody like
You used to make me smile
Sing a beautiful lullaby
Like Stay for a while
Can you play for me
Play a simple melody
Like you use to do
You were my rhythm and my blues
Can you play for me

Purify

BY ASHANTI FLEMISTER

Purify my mind so I could think pure thoughts
And keep my mind stayed on You
Purify me so that I could be at ease
Keep my mind stayed on thee

Purify my heart so I can love like you
Have mercy on others like you do
Purify my heart so that I could forgive
No longer hold grudges, and love shall win

Purify my body to be a living sacrifice
Holy and pleasing to Your sight
Purify me and release me from my chains
In you, I am no longer a slave to my old ways

Ready to Love

BY ASHANTI FLEMISTER

Verse 1 (Female Vocals)
I can be the one you need
I can be the one who's meant to be
With you, I'll give my everything
If you're ready
I will be your dream come true
And I promise I will stay with you
There's nothing in this world I wouldn't do
If you're ready

Chorus
If you're ready to love
I'll be the one you need
I'll give the best of me
Love you wouldn't doubt to trust
If you're ready to love
I'll be the support in your life
I'll stand right by your side
Love that you've been dreaming of
If you're ready to love

Verse 2 (Male Vocals)
I'm ready to put away the games
Around my boys, I feel no shame
Whenever you need me
You could call my name because I'm ready
I will be the strength in your life
And I promise, girl
I will always treat you right
Whatever you want, I will provide
Because I'm ready, baby

Chorus
Girl, I'm ready to love
I'll be the one you need
I'll give the best of me
The man you wouldn't doubt to trust
Because I'm ready to love
I'll be the backbone in your life
I will stand the test of time
Love that you've been dreaming of
Because I'm ready to love

Bridge
I am ready to love you forever and ever
(Female Vocals) I'm going to love you forever and ever
I am ready to love you. We will stay together
(Male Vocals) We will stay together forever and ever
I am ready to love you forever and ever
I am ready to love you
We will stay together

Chorus
(Female vocals) If you're ready to love, I'll be the one you need
(Male vocals) I'll give the best of me
Love that you've been dreaming of if you're ready to love

So Amazing

BY ASHANTI FLEMISTER

I was raised in the church a long time ago
Knew about Your name as the pastor said so
I did not know the true meaning of having a relationship with You
You opened my eyes, and then I knew

Remember the time that I cried out Your name
So sick of my life
Alone with great pain
Struggled with my mother not being there like she should have
Sought out to find love in men but no one could have

Loved me the way that I needed to be loved
Knocked on every door but there was no one
I didn't think that anybody out there could save me
You came into my heart, and then You made me

A better woman
A woman of standard
You taught me how to love myself
And my life would get better

You reminded me that I was fearfully and wonderfully made
And there was nothing too hard for You
You will always make away

Every battle that I face now is no longer mine
All things are possible in Your appointed time
Life without You Lord
Please, You're better than life itself
It's so amazing that You want me to be prosperous and in health
The peace that You give me surpasses all understanding
That's why walking with You Lord is so amazing.

So You Say You Are a Christian

BY ASHANTI FLEMISTER

I can't explain the heaviness in my spirit
Once again, I'm going through but
You don't want to hear it
You point the finger as if perfection is in your DNA
You have the mindset of holier than thou
Been when exposed, you have nothing to say

So, sit down, shut up, and part your lips
To something useful like prayer
Where is the love saints
Some of you act like unbelieving haters

So, you say you're my sister and brother in Christ
But as soon as I do wrong
You're screaming out crucify
You can't win souls if you can't show

Love within the kingdom
Get your nose out of the clouds
Your human, and it's just that simple

All of us are accountable for our own actions

By the dwelling of our Holy Spirit
But when I do wrong and convicted
From you, I don't want to hear it
So, quit Tweeting and Facebooking as if

You were already called up in the rapture
One thing is for sure
We Christians need to get it together
Let us really show that the church is better than the club
My question to you saints is
Where is the love

Sweet Memories

BY ASHANTI FLEMISTER

Hershey was the color of his smooth
Beautiful dark brown skin
Still in the daze from those sweet memories of
Way back when he used to care
I had the pleasure to embrace his tender touch
His soft-spoken words from his full pillow lips
seems to be enough
To put me in a trance as I dance
And reminisce about the past
That time when he was considered to be mine
I often prayed that it would last.
Unfortunately, things didn't work out
And we decided to go on two different paths
Yet I still get chills up my spine
Every time I am in his presence
With fantasies and dreams that we two are destined to be
So, I hold these sweet memories locked up deep inside
Being careful that my emotions won't deceive my mind
If I could only see his smile

That would ultimately satisfy me
As I sit back and reminisce on those sweet memories

Teach Me

BY ASHANTI FLEMISTER

When I thought I was alone
You were there to comfort me
When death looked me in the eyes
You were there to protect me

You wouldn't let me go
Despite the times that I've failed
Oh, how I am so glad I know You well

Whenever I was down
You lifted me up
When I wanted to give in
You told me to never give up

With all this in mind
I feel like I owe You my life
My body as a living sacrifice
Although I know Your grace
There are some things that I do that still causes you pain

I want to let it go, but I seem to run into the same thing
Please take this away, Jesus
Because I don't want to continue
To say forgive me, Lord
Then turn around and deceive You

I desire to be real and do what's pleasing in Your sight
So that others would want to have Christ in their life
As Psalms 143 reads
Teach me to do Your will

For You are my God
May Your good spirit
Lead me to level ground
Create in me a clean heart
And renew in me a right spirit within me
I desire to please You Lord
So please...teach me

That's Why

BY ASHANTI FLEMISTER

Thank you, God, for sending Your son, Jesus
Because when He came into my heart
Life had just begun
My battles I go through
Are no longer mine
I can do all things through my Savior Christ
That's why
I dedicate this poem to you
For all the things you brought me through
You made a way of escape
This poem is for you today
Everyday life has its own trouble
In this worldly system
Your mind is tempted to think double
But if I draw near to you
The enemy will flee
I wrote this poem to you
So that the world would see
That I can't imagine how life would be

If you weren't in the equation
Low self-esteem, complacency, followed by depression
Can't forget where I came from
Or where I'm going
I thank you, Jesus, for being a part of my story

There Is Work To Do

BY ASHANTI FLEMISTER

Wounded from the depths of my soul to
The very thoughts of my brain
Hurt from the top of my head
To the soles of my feet

I feel defeated
But I can't stay there
I have a special friend named Jesus
Who told me to get up

And that's all I needed
There is work to do
Although I felt defeated
I wanted to give up

He told me to move
Because there is work to do

Crazy things that I had experienced
Nobody's fault but mine

Yielded to my downfall
I could have respectfully declined
But no need to beat myself

It's time to move
Because there is work to do
I'm blessed by my mishaps
Because now I have a story to tell you

Wounded...get up
Betrayed...get up
Broken...get up
Depressed...get up.
Move...there is so much work to do

These are the Times

BY ASHANTI FLEMISTER

These are the times that we must believe or deny
That Jesus is Lord
This is a war Cry
It's time for God's people to be strapped with His word
Jesus is coming, but we still act like we haven't heard
We have to be separate with no compromise
Be holy because He is holy because these are the times
Men being with men and women being with women
Kids having kids and being disobedient
These are the times
Where recession is on high
Collecting pennies to feel are gas tanks
To get from the North to the Southside
These are the times
For God's people to be set apart
Stand up and stand out
This is a war cry
Get ready for the battle because
These are the times

To Be Continued...

BY ASHANTI FLEMISTER

Chillin by myself
Enjoying the sweet melodies of silence
In a completely calm state
The flow of energy is balanced

Counting on my blessings
That the Lord has bestowed upon me
Looking back at my past with a smile
Fast forward to the joys of victory

Can't front though
Because in the midst of chill
Sometimes I wonder if the Lord will send
Me the one for real

I have accomplished all these things
Just me, myself, and the Master
Wonder if Prince charming will come
Will there really be a Happily Ever After

Not ashamed to say that sometimes
Being held is like a nice solace groove
I'm cool with chilling by myself
But sharing my world with Love
Hmmm, to be continued....

To the Love of My Life

BY ASHANTI FLEMISTER

To the love of my life
My shining star
I want you to know that I'm here for you
near or far

Even thru the storms when we are
Vulnerable to make mistakes
Have no fear, my love
because in my heart, you will always have a place

Only God knows if we were really meant to be
Hold fast and don't let go because, in time, we will surely see
Let's take one day at a time and see far this will go
I may be yours forever if you say so

Truth and the Light

BY ASHANTI FLEMISTER

I was covered with shackles
Burdens burying me alive
Called on my friends, but they all passed me by

I'm screaming for mercy
Lost and want to be found
I called on my family
But there was no one around

So, I had a talk to Christ
Who is the truth and the light
He said you won't find truth
Until you give me your life

Jesus said, pick up your cross
And follow me
My life hasn't been the same
Since I've been walking with Him

Truth Hurts

BY ASHANTI FLEMISTER

Can we really get mad at our men if we continue to
invest years in a relationship without a wedding ring
and to spazz out and feel ashamed
when he decides, he calls it quits
and finds someone more fit
To wear his last name

I'm not throwing any shade if that's your thing
but I desire a solution to end our emotional pain
Are we really sick and tired of being sick and tired
We say that we want to meet our King
but are we doing what's required

I looked at my reflection today and realized
That I have work to do
to no longer chill on my pity
and cry another boo hoo
if I continue to give my body and soul away to fools
I'm taking a stand to be my own best friend

And to treat myself well
Nobody can do it better than myself

Uniquely You

BY ASHANTI FLEMISTER

You are the definition of beautiful
Fearfully and wonderfully made
As God predestined you to be
Others may not understand your uniqueness
Because they have to be connected with the Most High
To fully comprehend your greatness
You have a heart for God
Living out His purpose and plan
Staying focused, full speed ahead
Keep going, my friend
Who cares if nobody else understands
Continue to obey God's commands
Jesus is holding you in His hands
Submit all of your pain and hurt to Him
Be set free, release, and breathe
Proceed with your dreams
And watch them come true
I wish that you could see
What I see in you

Believe in yourself
As I believe in you

Walking by Faith

BY ASHANTI FLEMISTER

As you walk into your destiny, the waves of life may come to distract you. It may even knock you down. I encourage you to get up back up, wipe the dust off, and be refreshed and renewed by God's unfailing love and strength. Destiny is ahead...victory has your name on it....

The way that I am

BY ASHANTI FLEMISTER

Here are my flaws
Here are my addictions
Here are my mistakes
Here are my wrong decisions

I'm coming to you the way that I am
Is that what you said
Because that's what I heard
And that's what I read

Here are my bad habits
Here are my sins
Here are my transgressions
How can I even begin

I'm coming to you the way that I am
Is that what you said
Because that's what I heard and
That's what I read

Will you still love me
Despite the real me
Could it be possible
That you will accept me

If I come to you the way that I am
Because I don't deserve you
I don't fill fit to serve you

But every bright morning
You give me tender mercies
Embrace me with blessings
So I lift my hands with praise and Thanksgiving

What is love?

BY ASHANTI FLEMISTER

Love is an unexplainable feeling
It is an eternal flame that burns
with deep meaning

The flame will never go out
no matter the circumstance
Until death do us part, it will always last

Many people have mistaken love with lust
But when the lust is gone
love wouldn't mean as much

When it's real love
Lust won't have to be the case
When love and lust are competing
Love always seems to win the race

Who Really Cares

BY ASHANTI FLEMISTER

.

Who would be my life support to revive me
When my world is being tossed upside down
Who can I run to or turn to
Would there be anybody around

I just want to live
I just want to breath
If it wasn't for my faith in God
Who gives me strength

I would be done
Walk a mile in my shoes
Are you ready to this length?

I'm tired of defending myself in relationships
Trying to stay ahead of the game
I would like to demolish the walls
Let a man love me unconditionally

With no shame
Put respect on my name
And I do him just the same

We don't have to be perfect
Just learn each other and grow
Have each other's back and let love take control

You've been So Good to Me

BY ASHANTI FLEMISTER

Oh Lord, how awesome is Your Name
No other I could claim
Although some days get rough
In You, I still will trust
So glad I know You well
Can't keep it to myself

I will tell it to my family
Tell it to my friends
Tell it to the whole wide world
How good you've been
You've been so good to me

Oh Lord, Your name deserves the praise
With You, I'm not afraid
You said You'll never leave
A promise You made to me
All things are possible
Through You, it's incredible
Your Word will never fail

Can't keep it to myself

I will tell it to my family
Tell it to my friends
Tell it to the whole wide world
How good you've been
You've been so good to me

Your Love

BY ASHANTI FLEMISTER

Verse 1
Still blessed from the day that I came in the light of You
You are my peace
My reason I make it through
Passion it comes from you up above
Nobody's love can compare to Your love

Chorus
It was Your love that lifted me
It was Your love that set me free
It was Your love that made a change in my life
It was Your love that made everything right
Nobody's love but the love of Jesus
It was Your love
Your precious love

Verse 2
I remember the time when I was lost and confused
My friends weren't around
My family was through

Peace I could not find
No sunny days
Until you came into my life
And wiped my tears away
No longer have to depend on things outside of Your hands
No substance or mankind could help me understand that
You are the reason I breathe
The reason why faith goes beyond what I see

Repeat Chorus

About the Author

Ashanti Flemister is a Columbus, Ohio native who is poet, photographer, actress and singer, and songwriter. Ashanti has also been a photographer since 2016 and is the CEO of her company called Moments Tayken LLC. She uses her poetry and photography platforms as creative outlets to express herself and to also encourage and empower others.

Ashanti had obtained her bachelor's degree in Psychology from North Carolina A&T State University in 2005 and is currently working on her Master's in Social Work at the Ohio State University. She is currently an active member of the Zeta Phi Beta Sorority Inc. where she enjoys making a difference in the community.

instagram.com/moments_taykenpersonally

CPSIA information can be obtained
at www.ICGtesting.com
Printed in the USA
BVHW070004230221
600780BV00009B/903

9 781950 719686